D1245431

A ROOF GONE TO SKY

POEMS

Kathleen McCann

Carpenter Gothic

Carpenter Gothic Press

Published by Carpenter Gothic Inc.

Box 714 Island Heights, N.J. 08732

ISBN: 09668739-3-9

Carpenter Gothic
440 Beacon Ave
Beachwood, NJ 08722

Cover design and painting: Vincent Crotty

ACKNOWLEDGMENTS

Poems in this collection originally appeared in the following publications:

American Writing: "The Ferry"
Aura Literary Review: "The Mourner's Bench"
Blueline: "Cather's Cottage, Grand Manan Island, N.B., Canada"
Blue Unicorn: "Thoor Ballylee"
California Quarterly: "After Skating at Cranberry Pond"
The Comstock Review: "The Small Hours"
Crow: "When New England's Ship Comes In"
Descant: "Country of Warnings," "Drumcliff Yard," "The Connor Pass, County Kerry"
Fan Magazine: "Teaching the Cat To Catch"
Interim: "Up the Ante," "Things Women Say To Feel Safe," "Witness," published under the title "Pitch"
The Journal of Pastoral Care: "Laying on of Hands"
Matchbook: "Slea Head"
The Midwest Quarterly: "Reversing Falls"(published under the title "Wait For Me")
The Onset Review: "The Weight of it"
Opus Literary Review: "Entrances and Shadows" (published under the title "Still Life")
Pacific Review: "Sanitarium: Bucze, Poland, January, 1958"
Paws & Tales: "No More Dog Poems"

Pegasus: "Austin Unit, the Old Boston State Hospital Grounds"
Piedmont Literary Review: "Nine Holes, Sligo"
Portland Review Literary Journal: "Primer"
Potato Eyes: "The Poet Sells the Business"
Riverwind: "Powder Point," "Inside the Slaughterhouse Gate, Tralee"
Sojourner: "Falling Backwards Through My Life," "Rainwatcher"
The Sonoma Mandala Literary Review: "Irish Coins," The Connemara Pony," "Lough Caum"
Sou'wester: "Comforts"
Sulfur River Literary Review: "The Garden"
Tucumcari Literary Review: "Morning Table"
Whiskey Island Magazine: "Apparition"
Wisconsin Review: "A Roof Gone to Sky"
Worcester Review: "Shackford Street"
Writer's Forum: "School for the Infirm, Sligo"
Xavier Magazine: "The Grandmother Who Lived with Us"

With deep gratitude I wish to thank Winston Bolton and Faye George for their scrupulous care and attention with these poems.

Barbara de la Cuesta, for faith in *A Roof.*

And finally, to my friends and family; you are here, always.

~ for **Carla**

For thou my lips may breathe adieu,
I cannot think the thing farewell.

- Tennyson
"In Memorium"

~
Teresa
~
whose *singularity* delighted us

Contents

V1.   Country of Warnings

Whatever furrow you dig in the red earth,
Whatever the tree you hang your lights on,
There comes that moment
When what you are is what you will be
Until the end, no matter
What prayer you answer to ~ a life
Of margins,   white of the apple, white of the eye,
No matter how long you hold your arms out.
You glance back and you glance back.

- Charles Wright

1

Entrances and Shadows

Morning Table

The butter lies in its boat.
Plants take their place.
Pine cones, a tray of sea shells,
part of the arrangement.

Summer – beyond the window
in a yard flush with growth,
dandelions and plenty of green –
pleases the eye.

I take my coffee out
to the little table.
Sitting amongst color and bees, I arrange
to feel good.

Entrances and Shadows

Each night I walk my dog. Our house
waits at home full of light with two
cats sitting by the door till we enter
again their life of spaces, nooks, entrances and shadows.

But they have never stood as she and I
at our last tree, where each evening we look
upward to what the moon has given us.
How much light across the apples,
if any at all; how much fruit?

Reversing Falls

If I move slowly over the path
down to the water,
act as if getting there
matters little at all,
dawdle getting out of the car,
finish out the song, wait
for the next one to come on,
stare up at the big woods
waiting for my climbing feet,
coffee gone, cup dead in my lap,
maybe then

the lone egret,

just now preparing to lift off
the back waters, out over falls
that reverse on themselves, beyond
a strong current and tan
marsh grass,

will drop his spread of wings,
pull in,
and wait for me.

Walking the Beach on Valentine's Day

Yes, we bring our hearts,
and some bread for the gulls and ducks
who call this peninsula home.
As fast as I throw it out
my dog shoots off.
Keep things for yourself: his credo.

Love sounds its own bell.
I see it, in the corner
of his eye.

Feel it,
rise up
through me.

Shackford Street

The house is empty
except for the houseguest
writing at the kitchen table.

And the dog, waiting to go out,
hungry for woods
even in sleep.

Drinks in the yard this afternoon,
out in the red chairs; summer talk.
Light on the long-shadowed lawn.

Apparition

Everything goes to seed around you.
House, barely standing,
standing behind.
Faint path, once a driveway,
hemmed by vine
grown to running the place.

And you sir, neither
coming nor going
midway on that wild lawn,
rake resting on the heart,
hands cupped round,
lighting up.

This, the only life we know.
A stooped old man taking
pleasure in his pipe at dusk...

a jogger, five miles out,
chanting under her breath,

no one lives here
no one could.

Laying on of Hands

When another's hands are beyond reach,
soothe your own brow; rub trouble away.

Stroke the head you daily argue with,
touch with the same tenderness

offered others. Then call upon
your faith, if only the size

of a mustard seed, measure enough,
pin money in the cupboard's cup.

Evening Prayer

One by one Unitarians assemble
behind solid black doors
that lock out the sea.
Business: greeters for summer residents,
committees to drum up new blood.
Maybe they argue, fettered to petty gripes.

Meanwhile the sky has its say.
Clouds erased, blue
headed back to black.
Slow, sweet slip of day,
its one wish dispatched:
to be taken as is.

Petition

And after each day's mumbled requests
spoken in the roots of back alley vines
and good neighborhoods too,
we ask only that you hear us.

We, who walk this earth, or climb
through oil, grease, and fractious streets,
ask only that you forgive, and pardon
our groping ways, remembering you school
the lame, the dumb, the sightless.

A Roof Gone to Sky

Low-tide at Este's Bluff. Dulse.
Mottled strips of slithery purple
picked and brought up between tides
by those who don't mind muck,
the climb down.
The old cannery – rusted tin lids
bleeding onto grass,
grass breaking floorboards –

is home to me. I sit
eyeing the world
through a gaping hole
that once held glass.
Wracked by the elements,
half the roof gone to sky,
my ragged barn,
close to giving in.

Austin Unit,
the Old Boston State Hospital Grounds

Long since closed,
a building falls to ruin.
A crumbling walkway leads
to unattended trees
barring the main door.
Birds have made a home here.
Across the peeling,
institutional green
of caged porches,
on the first day of spring
in air a little cool,
there is singing.

Powder Point

Let us have both:

Crows, high in the blue air,
bitching, jeering above tamped-
down marsh grass and bland tide;

denial through the familiar,
the sound of a rake pawing the earth,
each pull whispering

all is well
all is well.

11

Primer

The Poet Sells the Business

Everything must go.
House, barn, all the acreage you see,
much more down back.
Places I never get to.

This morning I saw a blue heron
hugging the pond's shore.
Shy bird, ice-still, resigned to solitude.
For a moment I thought to rescind my offer,
not climb the worn path back
to meet you, waiting on the porch step.
I thought to put this bird in a story.
Sit by the pond, pin the thin
slate-blue of him.

No, it all goes.
With a few good years left,
I'm getting out.

Primer

Without instruction how would any of us
steady the hand of love? There, on the wire
over the small yard, birds line up.
But where does the bread come from?
You have been away a long time, hand-
held, let go at the door, free to turn
what feels a stiff key and step in.
Breathe deep.
Rugs beam up at you; plants have been kept.
The cats, though a little fat, are fine.
This is your home, ring in a brave toast.
Be well. Birds pass at the window.

Teaching the Cat To Catch

We start with grounders, anything
an average infielder could get.
Our incremental drills capitalize
on youthful enthusiasm (his)
till the bed doubles as a trampoline
for pop-ups.

The kid's a natural.
That's what you get for having dogs for years.
When I lay cross-country skis over
two chairbacks to wax them, my late
labrador's face appears, his rippling body
gaga for the woods.

The little rookie with phenomenal reach
supine against the bathtub's curved
warning track, winks,
nods to the mound
and steals.

Cows, Headlines & the 4th

Nothing to do,
ever.
Except promenade under dawn's auspices,
bring forth a day's worth of light
packed in those hefty, speckled sides.
Later, curtsy beneath the stand of maples
whisking them toward home and
dinner.

Let fireworks crackle in Amherst's
hot sky!
Tomorrow, unabashed,
back by popular demand,
the cows will tromp out,
headlining under that same roof:
doing the old soft-shoe
of another day.

The Jobs

Some last a month, a week,
a couple of days.
She packs Christmas packages at Hickory Farms
in the basement.
Standing on line beside the owner's retarded son,
she arranges little squares of cheese and meat
over the green Easter filler paper. Sprinkles
a few strawberry candies over the whole thing.
Too erratic. This is the year she found crystal meth.
She quits before they fire her.

Witness

Gun shot in the woods.
My dog kicks, eyes
wide, ears pricked.

I imagine blood running
from his side. Eyes
milky with love, blank.

My witness, these crows,
Mayors of the high,
thin-branched pines,

staring down, always
bitching, tough-
skinned,
no pitch for grief.

The Grandmother Who Lived with Us

Why this morning do I remember
the day you stood calling me
from the back porch?
Frail, bad eyes, no strength for much,
you always wanted something.
I climbed the blighted remaining apple tree,
high as the branches would hold,
looked out past roofs, high-tension wires,
where the ocean met with sky,
knowing you never left the porch.
That one day you did:
gimping across the grass,
cane thrust above your head,
you were out for me.
Taunting you, full of a family's venom,
I lowered down to the crotch of the tree
to the painted-on ring of creosote –
black marking the ghost of a hacked off limb –
took aim at your unsteady feet;
bitter as the fruit I hurled.

Things Women Say To Feel Safe

Like bye-bye, syrupy,
slithering, always hurriedly
off the tongue.
Take this woman, exiting
the library's revolving door
into a bright world.
She is safe, *bye-bye* smeared
over the check-out librarian,
book clutched to her breast,
scarf tossed back, jaunty
sure steps toward the car.

No More Dog Poems

No more head-hung
thin-shouldered
drooping
down in the mouth

slinking off
with a meatless-
skimpy-excuse-for-a-bone
dogs.

Every third line or so,
skulking in or bowing out,
eyes flooded with fear.
If speech were theirs –

fat sorries would fill the air.
My dogs – pitiful eyes,
long-stricken faces –
truth is, I need them.

Call it what you will:
unfinished business,
projection,
metaphor for my wound.

All I know is
each time I whistle
they come running,

round the corner,
nudge for the dole,
my habitual handout.

Rainwatcher

"On looking up he saw Georgia at a window, watching the rain
come down in sheets, as it does in Texas."

- A Woman On Paper, Anita Pollitzer

She watches the storm, hard-driving, coming out of
        nowhere,
pelting the dirt road out front.
No wonder we say those things: *teeming,* or
in sheets.
It's not the rain sends her scurrying
from the screen door, retreating
within the old beach trailer.
But lightning, out over the ocean
unzippering sky.
And a week's worth of fitful sleep,
dreams that take a forty-year-old woman back
to a father's hands unfastening his belt.
She thinks of Georgia.
Young, self-assured, standing at the window,
illumined by the glow of early career.
Good at being herself in a world favoring men.
Paying attention to everything,
leaving nothing alone.

Up the Ante
for Marny Muir

I like to think of you
bending over some find
at the beach.

Head down, attentive
to minute detail.
Always a therapist

even at play. But that's
not true. Or fair.
High roller

who loves to throw,
sweeten the pot,
charm away a bad hand.

Quit while you're ahead?
Fat chance. Lover
of the close dance.

Cather's Cottage,
Grand Manan Island, N.B., Canada

What years you must have spent here,
claiming it as yours, mixing
with the locals,
becoming an islander,
summers at a time.

I picture you coming over,
taxiing from Town Wharf,
traveling up in back
to Whale Cove.

You never did get away.
I saw the desk
in the tiny museum at White Head.
Manila card reading: *Desk on which*
Cather typed her manuscripts.

Riding the ferry rail,
tired, the long commute,
you must have known
it would end in work.

Inside the Slaughterhouse Gate, Tralee

Do animals have souls?
a child might ask.
The child would tire
standing where the sun
washes a truck down
slanting off its sides,
its rails where one pig
chews and nips.
A child would want
to find the center
of town, shops with candy.
Where does the soul go
when we die
and who has one?
Who, like these,
grunting and buckling
in a dark interior,
blinking shyly
when I move close.

111

When New England's Ship Comes In

Great Esker Park, North Weymouth

Dog, black setter, huge walrus,
Buddha of low tide.
Mysteries for you are not shells, nor meditation
in afternoon.
Purist, in love with air, the feel for mire.

In three months it will be November.
How we advance into time like a living sepia
deep and brown in body.
One day I will push dust away to remember this
particular dog.
Like looking at a Currier & Ives. Peace will abide,
the old mill pond.

It Works
for Liz

I mean winter
is falling
out of March &
spring just landed in
April & crocuses are
coming up
more birds are around & ducks
are returning to ducks
who didn't go.
My friend the artist always
asks – *does it work?*
And I never know what to say
but I understand this &
it does.

Old Labrador in the Sun

No pride!
Fat walrus, plunked
out here on this, your
afternoon bed of yard
for all the world to see.

Dreams, if you do own any,
must pass the eye,
nestling damp, dark earth
beneath your heaving body.

Carried on the breath
of voluminous snorings –

good dreams,
all good dreams.

Flurries

You were not even alive
when lightning split
the family cow in two.
Old Tess, falling
through her life
somewhere in the Midwest.

Now you tell that story here.
A true New Englander, waiting
with the rest of us for snow.
Straining, heads up,
willing gray clouds
closer,

we ask for presence,
that moment of clarity
before an event.
Flurries…
like circus,
come to town!

When New England's Ship Comes In

Nothing exists between August's hay mown
fields and winter's iron trap, but time.
Time, that slow, sweet slippage that drops the spoils,
days so rarified we wish them no end.

August is summer's brake, carousel's last
turn before the close.
What else can May do but pace, frantic
on the widow's walk, lilacs in hand?

After Skating at Cranberry Pond

So cold the hands burn,
fingers: numb-white.
Touch hurts.
My mother takes off my mittens
and lays them, nubby with ice,
on the kitchen radiator.
I give my hands over, place them
in the warmth of hers.

Palms up, my mother accepts my offering
and takes my small-boned hands
into her own.
I am the middle child, the tom-boy,
last one home.
I am the one who makes her stand calling
at the back door night after night
in a voice pitching anger.

I am the child she stoops to now,
the one returning her skates
to their nail over the cellar stairs.
The one running back,
eager, driven,
for those hands.

38

IV

Mercies

Comforts

If it is true that we are each character
churning through the long night's water,
then neither shows any remorse.

Nothing from Mary but a surfeit of hope
for more time, comfortable surroundings
to do, as so well she does, her choice part.

Martha cries only for organization,
cupboards in Corian, a new window
to let the world intrude on her duties.

At night they lie down closer
than any dream could bring them, twinned
spirits, nowhere but together to go.

Reading the Psalms at No One's Expense

If there is any comfort to be had
after the killing of children
and nameless others,
give it to us now.

Give us honey for the cup, balm
that means more than money,
armies, livestock,
and legends.

Grant us that promised mercy,
outstretched hand that bears
not root, nor blood from the tongues
of our dogs, but olive branch.

Grant that our names
be in the book of the living
so we may continue
combing the Word with our rakes.

The Weight of it

O God, the inky night spends itself.
No one here, not even a dream.
The world might not exist
except for this thin-boned hand's
compliant reach.
You know it well.
How can you bear
its touch?

Stepping Forth

Is there movement forward,
or is it only the seasons
rustling the bush, our
world beating its wings?

Who dares curb the urge
to blossom? Purled
desire cannot rest
until the earth
lets it go.

Mercies

The dog follows the country road and finds
a home. Marbled rottweiler, king of the pond,
   "We will call him Phillip," the couple says.
We take communion in the little cottage,
remember together the world's brokenness,
forget nothing: whom we have hurt,
who has harmed us.
Only love stands in for what came before.
Fire's hypnotic dance chides, *forgive,*
and let go expectations.
Did the country house expect five dogs?
The broken woman...love so late?
Kindness, or maybe grace, swings from a hinge
no hand can hold.

Next Year

Easy to believe what we love
comes back to us.
Something to revisit,
start toward again.

The cottages our eyes rely on:
Sea Breeze, Stay Awhile,
tell us we arrive, the coast's
coastal blur.

Count back the years
then to now,
now till then.
Again.

V

The Small Hours

Falling Backwards Through My Life

The heart is a fist,
a catcher's mitt not come
for, left for rain and sun
to beat on.
Persistent stammer,...*but*
but...catch phrases
in the body's lining,
the armor of want.
Backwards tonight,
twisting and falling,
Alice through the hole.
Tightwad,
the heart is a fist.
Oh, full, fat heart,
how your break me
with your wily
ways, how
you break me.

The Luck Letter

This letter has been sent to your for good luck. It has gone around the world nine times. The luck has now been sent to you. Your good fortune will come within three days of receiving this letter, provided you, in turn, sent it on. This is no joke.
Praise St. Jude!

Dear St. Jude,

    I know you are very busy, however,
I write to you today in regard to a letter
which I received.
If you will, allow me to refer to it
as, 'The Luck Letter.'
This letter purports to bring on good luck
provided the receiver makes twenty copies &
sends them on to friends and associates
within four days.
After a few days, the letter states,
you'll get a surprise, even if not
superstitiously inclined.
St. Jude, at this time in my life,
I'm leery of surprises.
Have just begun yet another job,
the hours of which fit nicely around
my writing schedule.

And isn't this poet business hassle enough?
You know what I'm sayin'?
But, there's the matter of this letter
with its serious, unsettling, contents
arriving in my mailbox today.
Gene Welch of the Philippines lost his wife
after receiving the letter. Of course he did fail
to send it on. $ 7,755,000 came his way later,
but sill in all, no wife.
And what about poor Carlo Danditto, an office
    employee,
he received the letter, had all good intentions
of sending it on, but failed to make
the ninety-six-hour deadline. He lost his job.
St. Jude, I mean to be frank with you,
again, I appreciate how busy you must be,
I will be brief.
It's Dalon Fairchild has me worried silly.
He received the letter only to scoff at it
then pitch it out. Sure, the great guffaw.
Nine days later he died. Died!
Jesus, St. Jude!

The Garden

How eagerly the branch accepts the wind.
The ice cream parlor chairs accept morning's light.
The poodle looks pleased with her cut,

the barn-red bird finds the farther tree.
Jean's patio lives on.
What is there to find displeasure in?

What else is there to mean by going home?
Except to touch once more the toe to dew;
and like the grass, allow the light its story.

Sanitarium: Bucze, Poland, January, 1958
for Jadzia

Monument to sturdiness, ark of a building,
dank, austere.
On stone-cold steps leading up the front walk,
a mother bends to kiss her child's cheek.
Lamb of a girl, six years old, thin, tubercular,
pressed against a grimy window pane
watching the world swallow her mother.

For years she will forget what happened.
Night sweats, night terror, the image
of a dim light swaying sends her back.
Over these stones, back through that wide-mouthed
door, down long halls, past a meager kitchen,
a room flickering under the shadow of one bulb:
a little girl,
alone in the corner of the room,
undressing, stepping out of her panties.
Looking up, the sweetest face,
full of questions, years on her tongue.
                    Where will I sleep?

The Mourner's Bench

The wind in the field sings
to the seated one, brushes back her hair,
moves silently over pursed lips fixed
on the work of mourning.

No hand could carve the flesh of this place,
chisel beneath the knotted wood
bent and creased with age, tears.
No heart could fail to distinguish

the sound that breaks forth
from her mouth
to wail
at the throaty sky.

The Small Hours

In everyone there is a wilderness of want.
No tribe exists that did not claim it all.
Open the fist and you will find
another growing in its place,
curling into itself like a wave,
eager to feel the penny in the palm;
flesh meets flesh.
How hard one must work uncurling desire,
the forced grip, cavernous need.
The shadow of the hourglass combs the wall,
brilliance in a certain time of day,
photographer's light.
Half way around the world children dive
for tourists' coins, polished charmers
who pour it on, more for the family at home.
Behind them, the blue-green agate water,
shimmering backdrop for these acrobats
who climb the oil-smeared pilings all day.
Non-judgmental, the water only watches.

V1

Country of Warnings

Irish Coins

Hosts of the harp and proud animals.
The Irish love to travel – if not far,
far enough in all the renditions.
Soil kept them here, rows and rows
to account for, produce from, maintain.
Take this old man, leaving the barn door,
his son behind him. Up and down the long rows
guiding the machinery.
This is ours their eyes say:
that recognizable proud posture.
My Aunt Ann had it: a timid slip
of a woman who squeezed my arm
hello saying, "How are ya," parting her lips,
a thin version of a smile.
No wonder Lucky their dog grew family
famous for his bared teeth –
rack of whites. There was a smile.
My aunt was timid unless telling a story:
if it involved travel, all it took.
Another woman sat in front of me
fingering the china plate, eyes transfixed
beyond the tea cup.

We just kept going and going, she'd say,
and finally we were in New York.

All the McNeils packed in the '57 Chevy,
sticky July, the middle of the night.
Then we just turned around and came home.

So that's it. Like the two
farmers attending their soil,
enough to know the back door exists,
kitchen with its ticking clock,
a fire if it is cool,
and bed when it is time.

Country of Warnings

"Let me enter the history of the world, if only
to hold an apple."

- Molly Sweat

Where yellow irises lace fields
note: soil there is poor.

Where you find the white-staffed bog cotton
know that the turf lies underneath.

A round sign on the road: **Caution/Black Spot**
marks someone's death.

Politics aside – Look how the trees huddle.
No choice but submission to horizontal rain.

A cow with her calf asleep beside her
will always know this wet ground as home.

The canal behind the trees
carries the sea out to more sea.

61

Nine Holes, Sligo

In memory of my grandmother, Ellen Woodis

My childhood must have come from here.
Light like this, making its way across
the Atlantic, pooling in Boston Harbor,
only to leave again.
How much of our lives spent running,
the metronome taps: *loss, loss.*
The setter who follows will never die,
in my memory crossing these greens
long past his owner, past the course
plowed under when condos come.
There, in the light haloing my ball
hit well beyond the green, unafraid,
the young girl has not yet crossed the sea,
not yet loosed her foot forever
on this unfertile green.

Slea Head

If I could paint it, I would.
Right there, where two cottontails
cross the field in tandem,
under the nose of a sheep with her ewe.
A second ewe sleeps in the stone wall's shade,
protected from the tireless sea below.
Oh, that backdrop, milky mist
haunting Dingle's other side.
Gulls sweep the sky, always
those few to a seascape;
and way out, one white sail
lilting east, headed maybe for Inishvikallane.

The Connemara Pony

Sometimes, I see the look of him alone,
not stuck to his mother's side,
legs tapering to black hooves.
A wobbly sentry, standing and eating,
standing and eating,
occasionally bringing up a leg
to brush away a fly.

When he's had his fill he folds
those spindly legs underneath,
erasing from view the black wire-brush tail.
Eyes shut, little body down, cream crease
in clover. Now the wind takes over
with its subversive charm.

School for the Infirm, Sligo

The girl with my name insists on plucking
the pen from my shirtpocket.
But what can she, with a mind as rift
and wild as the shore this school sits on,
do with it?
Each weekday, arriving to such beauty,
seeing with the eyes and nothing else.
Dull and long must be her days,
not necessarily true.
Look how the mind appears to work
urging the fingers crawling my pen:
      make something for us; take us somewhere.

The Cottage, Castlegregory

A white-washed slab, someone's pint-sized
version of tranquility, foregoing an entire history.
A breeze quivers; bends and
breaks to accommodate the squat chimney,
a tarnished, fletched, tin roof.
Rivets, graceless but durable,
shimmer in the sun.
Built to last, like everything else
here in this close
country of warnings.
Even the fuchsia, rife and wild,
with its drooping red bells,
its luscious, flaming breast,
leans forward from the tiny yard,
sunlight belting down,
to claim its share
of notoriety.

Thrift

"The landscape is a limestone karst
with only thin patches of soil."

-Museum, Inis Mean

Four days walking crannied pastures,
peeping over stone to more stone, as much
as all New England, twenty-five hundred miles.
Flowers dab: cowslip, woodbine, gentian,
hawthorne and sea-pinks the Irish call thrift.
Takes an iron spine to bend rock's curved tube,
walk hidden from sight to chores –
maybe the tavern for a drop.
More than iron, it takes an economized soul
that can match history's force of bargaining
strength, even where harsh,
an island's pledge of faithfulness.

Drumcliff Yard

Run down, unspectacular
if it were not him who is buried here.
Both church and cemetery need repair.
Ben Bulben in the distance.
Low-hung clouds thin its presence,
magnificenct nevertheless.
A soft day, the Irish saying,
light drizzle.

A young man mows the field
fronting the cemetery, where little
groups of twos and threes,
instructed by the marker,
turn left at the church door.
There, terse fierce words
down forever
as he wrote them.

Thoor Ballylee

"I am writing at a great
wide trestle table which George
keeps covered with wild flowers.
And every room," he said,
"laid hold of her touch."

Single file we make our way
up those narrow, famous stairs.
My thoughts stray from the castle's charm
to its damp, bleak, claustrophobic feel,
drown out the video which tells each room's story,
winds us to the roof with its grand view.

How they must have sat over tea and
scones one evening, or brandy perhaps,
husband and wife, with two children to think of,
weighed the future, assessed the property's
disadvantages, its redeeming features.
A family arrives where father must write
his country's history.

I am troubled by the hands that ordered
these rooms, arranged and rearranged
so that another could reap
a life of the mind.

*For every artist someone is at work
in the kitchen.* Willa Cather said that,
knowing something about the business.

The Connor Pass, County Kerry

In the half light
distance means nothing.
What is to follow here,
roads? This country
should get some.

Beyond the hard luck
turns, the thin-
boned lifestyle,
something else:

blackbird, wood-
pigeon, acres
of light off
mountainous green,
wild fuchsia
down in a row;
a wild sea.

Travel

1

Identical navy-blue sloops touch
the piling's high water mark;
two masts spear an ominous sky
where gray on gray sweeps
the moon to nothing.
Gulls thread the burly sky, fretting
above the wild swans who dip and preen
in their elitist posture, indifferent
to the city's night life.
Galway's tour busses rest beside the channel.

The ferry returns from Inis Mean under
a pink yet somber sky spitting rain.
The names of horses jumping for a sixteen-
hundred-pound purse, their silhouettes sleek
against the sea, carry back over the water:

*Conemara Fai*r
Inishfree
Killybeg's Son

I see the Irishman at the boat's rail,
his city's landmarks in his eyes, eyes
like my grandmother, who came from Galway.

11

Out of Ireland's west coast, the Burren's
marbled limestone, the glossy, textured roads
of Connemara to Clifden, white rock rises.
White mixed with marble until the eye tires,
until wet-bottomed bogs reflect nothing.
Rock, marble, memory:

> faint paths hemmed by vine,
> a clock's quiet hands on the bureau,
> houseguests in the kitchen,
> fields laced with iris,
> a rake resting on the heart,
> slate-blue of a story,
> creosote rings on the apple tree.

111

Where are the people I love now?
How many of those I called mine are left?

Every kind gesture comes back to us,
safe in the palm,
coins for the store at the corner.

Will ya run to the store, Kate?
I've been waiting on a few things.

1V

An Irishman at an A.A. meeting
breaks the record for foul language.
But sky at the window, playing out
a last hand before nightfall,
trumps.
A calm sea at the end of the street.

What this world offers to us:
bird-song flecked air, gorse,
wild iris on the hillsides, and
for our feet, innumerable paths
creased with needles the color
of rust, smelling like fire.

Lough Caum

Rising off the lake – the sound
of oars knocking – a stiff,
light breeze persists;
a handful of people fish.
One girl, suave in her knickers
and black velvet cap, reels in,
click over click, until her thumb
squeezes the brake on her rod.
She reaches for the wet line.
"Just a nibble," her words
carry back where I sit
with a book, *Irish History:
Then and Now,* unopened in my lap.

The Ferry

I am the crossing of all that you hold dear;
come to my rails bearing whatever you bring.
No night exists apart from this delivery.
From out of those hands, relaxing their
grip on the wrought-iron cold, let fall
silences tight as new berries,
aches having no place but deeper in.
    Too soon, too soon, the spirit whistles,
the light we know pinched away.

Kate McCann teaches poetry and American literature at Eastern Nazarene College in Quincy, Massachusetts. After studying poetry at Washington University and serving as pastor of a small church in Missouri, she has recently returned to her beloved Weymouth, Massachusetts where she lives a short walk from Boston's South Shore.